DISJOINTED

Tengushee Interactive

www.tengushee.com

Endless.

Foreword

You will find I don't have much use for poetic convention in this book. Indeed, this is why this collection has been so named **Disjointed**. It sits in stark contrast to a year of strict Haiku as published in my previous book September to September. Rest assured, I do know about poetry from many cultures... I have however in this instance, after careful consideration and self-education, chosen to ignore the rules almost entirely.

What's existence without minor acts of rebellion?

What's life without **mischief**?

Tengushee, 2019

This world is wrong

it is not where I am supposed to be

it drains from me

all that I am, need, feel and aspire to see

will I ever **be free**?

This space between the worlds

The time when I am here

But feel the call of there

These times are the loneliest

This time is the hardest

Before sleep takes me

I leave and I arrive

These times are the loneliest

These times are the loneliest

Cold bright **blinds my eyes**

neither winter nor summer

Autumn dulls my heart

Hope

Impermanence

Steal the day

Awakening

Spiders

Dark art and shadows

Endless

Message to the Lost

Somewhere between hope and fear is a fire inside

Your civil war of tears

Ends

Fear

The violin call

Chased by the magpie cackle

God is my tide

The spider and the fly

Hum

This is hell, and you're here forever

I'll do it, I'll do it all

Fire

Shadows are more than just shadows;

Hold me tight

Let us end our story.

Unhappy parents

attending an Autumn child's

dull birthday party

Because a truth is

universal, misery

does love company

Only the good die young

those who are satisfied

secure with what they've given

they don't fight the tide

Living longer is not the way

The vapid seek to extend their lives

with no idea for why

to watch yet more trash TV

cringing and afraid to die

Living longer is not the way

I build prisons for

myself from the **comfort** of

lone activity

The Internet has

now weaponized schadenfreude

consequence fetish

Shine light in darkness

walk with careful dignity

then light the fire

The genocide of

my kind was complete, we were

myths... **myths that saved you**

The record of our existence

is made eternal not by

the beasts hidden in our wardrobes,

not by the skeletons of our pasts,

or even the histories of our actions...

But by the **footprints we leave on the souls of others**.

In that way we shine glamorous

above them

and are immortal

The key to the signal is in the puppet

skull calls

The way to the signal is in the puppet

dream calls

The way to the signal is in the demon

dream calls

The way to the endless is in the demon

dream cries

The way of the endless is in the demon

dream cries

and **the poem never dies**.

I once was different
no more slack for the weak
who would blame me
their ally supporter and sponsor

I know no fear

I once was different
no more slack for the weak
who would shame me
their insecurity manifest in hate

I know no fear

I once was different
no more slack for the weak
who would maim me
abandon me and leave me alone

I know no fear
I once was different

Was it me?

Or was it my side

Was it right?

Or was it barbarous

The face distorted

The ramblings disjointed

The girls either side

The venom stabbed in organically

Spite, retribution and yet so procedural

His fate was no random act

He'll survive it for a time

We bring him pain

We decide when he dies

If.

Hope

Stolen

Promises long forgotten

lives separated by mundanity

regardless, I keep the balefire burning

The glorious mask of death come

shimmering in beautiful unreality

facing down all those who oppose

all those of nothing

what we became isn't who we are

Never started this way but here none the less

once glowing bright in the anarchy of youth

champion and saviour to all that knew

all those of something

what we become isn't who we were

isn't who we will be.

Disturbances shadow

unease in dreams and daylight

realms as one waiting

The moonlight, in your eyes

the night makes your soul decide

no love

just darkness

your fear

is you

Come the morning, come the daylight

will you **lay down by my side**

oh lord

my love

my life

is dark

Cry your weak heart out

blame them for the dark as you

fail to reach for light

Once you have loved deep and lost all

that depth of feeling

resonates only in memory

a faint heart wrenching echo

of a shadow long since passed

never to be felt again

treasured by the wise

lamented by the weak

souls bound forever

out of reach

She said if I could

have them **rue the day** I would

here comes the sunrise

I can only chase after

it west some more now my love

I heard screams from the night

in a dream in the night

they called to me

a wild hunt for me

an imperfect vision of a future written

Gone for now I have

not seen my **fox faced girl** since

the summer sunset

\---

It is not only

dead resting in the quiet

cold winter graveyard

Spiders scuttle, and

noble turtles lurch beneath

the **same trees, same moon**

Do not be troubled

by this life you lead it will

be over very soon

The twelfth is the darkest month
a past magical time of year
what once was here is hard to find
time made no room for dreams

... take the pathway back.

Now a time of mundanity
where commerce preys on you
reject it all with mischief
from the dark we see the light

... and we take the pathway back.

Hair can only be

so wet, once it is soaked then

you have zero to fear

Now we **go to war**

and your kin shall pay the price

for the games you play

Beneath the reckless

actions many a hoodlum

is **lost in love**

Promise that when you see the Samhain sunrise

you'll think of me

after all this time and forever more in perpetuity

you'll think of me

Promise that when the sun is high in the heavens

you'll think of me

of what was and what could have been somewhere in time

you'll think of me

Promise that when you feel the Samhain sunset

you'll think of me

the mischief the lust and the dark

Promise that when the bells toll for midnight

you'll forget

Haunted forever

by the Fae that should bring luck

prisoner of winter

Tired of the outside

alone but comfortable

is this right or wrong?

I tried to make them forget

I let them go, released them to their whims

They couldn't resist one last glance or hurrah

People are strange

Now they have gone there is some peace

Now the past is dust and they soar into their

Own air will they make it as who they should be?

People are strangers

The red eyed hounds.

They never fetch.

Remaining still as stone; gargoyles still amongst even the dead.
The only graveyard movement the flickering of the ghost,
framed by the mist, falling **between cracks in shadow and reality**
waiting to be whole again.

Waiting for escape from loneliness that never comes.

There is nothing more

frustrating than **magical**

creatures not being

The world is right

it is where you are supposed to be

it will feed you

give you all you need, all you could ever want

but you will never be free

Freedom lies beyond this world

freedom lies throughout the dreaming

freedom leads you to **the endless city**

Deep in the dreaming
where you exist when you don't
is a castle in clouds
miss it you won't

Deep in the castle
if you pry with some skill
is a book of dark truth
words that will kill

Deep in the book
you read what you fear
it's penned by your hand
that your end is near

I never cried for help
resigned to my fate
with commitment
and **faith**

and faith
with commitment
healed me once more
with a call of help

Take your time

it's yours

Take your time

let dreams mass

Take your time

plans run their course

Take your time

embrace this flow

Take your time

it is unending

Take your time

unstoppable

Take your time

impermanence stalks you

Take your time

swim within it

Take your time

all things converge

Take your time

see the labyrinth

The accidental

stright edge, reality and

magic with no crutch

Hide them from daylight

so in dark they run you wild

but never expect

that their promises be kept

because **wolves are born to lie**

Have you ever walked
between the cracks of the world
with the homeless, the lost or
the dammed, those who you look down
upon in fearful pity?

Have you ever stepped
from your path into a place
you don't recognise
unreal and full of danger
far removed from your comfort?

Have you ever lived
or simply been directed
from one safe space to
the next from one comfort to
another just pretending

Were you ever wild,
truly mad, lost or even free
or are you a fake
lying to yourself trapped
a bottled creature forever

Rolling hills of green

endless past the streams and brooks

a lone wooden lodge

home to three boys and a priest

ever in peace and harmony

While gathering food

one boy became lost in the

rolling hills beneath

azure clouds, and burning

sun, he ran and ran forever

Changing as he went

he became more **the heartbeat**

of a stallion

black horse thumping through his chest

in the real world eyes opened

Follow her here, and

there my **fox faced** girl is more

than she can admit

everything beneath the

shadow of the moon she says

I still chase her now

through dreams and wars and love, through

loneliness and joy

I see her in the distance

the edge of reality

The disco at the

end of the universe was

sublime and love with her true

a kiss beneath the coloured

lights and a promise to return

I never went back

took a step from dark to light

and never looked back

surrounded by new things now

alone I am enlightened

If you wish to gain

a person's full attention

you need but whisper

Always looking in

from the outside like I was

watching a **film of**

my life and studying the

plot without any emotion

Grim fear as a child

walking to school as if I

were walking to war

a natural state for a

lost creature in the wrong world

Seeking approval

from an **imaginary**

audience forever

Four am and mist

now covers everything

silence broken by

never ending ringing in

my ears fades to sleep and dreams

Mist **fading** as fresh

winter air awakens my lungs

bird song chatter all

around as time passes by

sunset fades blue to orange

You wake up in the

morning beneath beautiful

sunrise and are one

more step **closer to your death**

this will never not be true

Church bells and bird song

never fail to make me smile

life far from duty

Fae fire burns for real

justice in a world where the

law is made by men

Hell is losing the

path home, lost in the light and

longing for the dark

Alone once more I

ever wait for a while

set free from this world

no longer bound to it's law

us **forever together**

Pray before you sleep

fight before you die

live before you rest

fuck before you cry

Gods will see you wake

peace will be your life

death will be your rush

love will be your knife

Never hide your passion

Never cease to play

Never let them fall

Never leave the way

Faith wasted on the empty

naked together lost in comfort

cold lectures on vapid moral rights and wrongs

a glimpse of hot flesh in a faerie court

Mourning a belief in a distant lie

a taste of a forbidden sensual touch

memories of the lost tainted by your false saviour

heart so full so real so much

Reveal your pure beauty here,

Inside me, **my princess**. We make one

I as an outcast, you as seer,

Heroes journey run –

Fought the endless nothing,

We battle, live, love, die, roam

Fire shadow souls sing

The last to glimpse home

I always prayed to you, my saviour

Princess, my other half since gone

Like in ancient times, come to me,

As you have always done…

Reveal your relentless spirit here,

Inside me, **my ranger**. I risk all

Distant through honour and fear

We were ended by the rule –

Torn apart in space, in time

Left to be, but lost and alone

Our emotions considered a crime

Loves final fate flown

You always prayed to me, my saviour

Ranger, my completing half, my sun

Like long ago, then, grant this favour,

As you have always done…

I don't like goodbyes

no one should ever be forced

to **fly beyond reach**

Dreams my mind haunted

of late by the **ghosts of past**

emotion past lives

I only wish a future

where they are real not dreams

Storm is here again

please don't let me go again

half my soul again

please just take me home again

so we aren't alone again

Earth has mere minutes

to go, the last flame flickers,

our **fortune** dealt death

I remember the rush
the feelings and the smells
the slightest hauls me back
there to order once again

Lying in comfort is no
shield against the sharpest
of swords buried deep in
my memories heart

And although I try and try to start

No life is worth living
outside of the fray
no thoughts with having
now my duty has been done

Never know if I hate it
or I miss it, the line between
is so thin like a love
of hate, or a lust for heat, for hell

There is romance is the recollection of those who fell

On the worst days I
I wish I hadn't survived
and I wish I could have saved them
my fallen friends, their shattered souls

And I know I will never forget

the phantoms close and always

one moment behind my eyes,

I never lose my guilt, my ghosts, **my war**

I only lost their lives

No hiding for the

cowards who turned and ran away

The King comes for you

The war in heaven

I wish you could have seen it

I was who I was supposed to be

I am forever chasing myself

The war in the dreaming

I wish I could have saved them all

I was the line between you and the darkness

I am a survivor, first of the last

The war in my heart

I wish we'd had more time

I was so young and so lost

I am alone now

The war in my head

I wish I didn't have these memories

I was lost in the darkness

I am the **one who waits forever**

They'll tell you that lust is fleeting

those that never had the passion for it

They'll tell you that it fades with time

those that never had the heart for it

They'll tell you you'll forget about it

those that never had it

They'll tell you you'll move on

those that never moved an inch to begin with

They'll never understand

those that never lived

The truth is that

we all fight our own battles

most of them won't be worth the pain

but, some of them, some of them

will be **worth it all**

Hell on Earth began in 2015...

[Originally published on the murky depths of the World Wide Web in 2015]

Back in the 90's Cyberpunk was a slightly confused Willow O' The Wisp concept. The term had been co-opted by fashion, music, futurists, hackers and technologists all around the same time. In the true spirit of the punk part of the term there was no coherency, and no sense of organisation and no cult of dogma. It was a loose term to describe someone into the extremely diverse array of fiction that sported the term and or the aesthetic of those worlds they portrayed.

Fast forward to the present day.

The history of popular opinion now erroneously regards the 90's as a far more coherent time for a movement called Cyberpunk. After all so much of what we associate came from or was 'culted' at that time. As an example consider the movie and literary aesthetic of Cyberpunk, films like; Terminator 2, Hackers, Blade Runner, The Matrix etc. (the list goes on, exhaustively in many places online including http://cyberpunkonline.net/cyberpunkarchive) and all the works of Gibson, Jeff Noon etc. etc.

All of this work is heavily and consciously associated with Cyberpunk as a 'movement in retrospect', in truth many aspects of those films do not fit at all with the underlying themes (or one another), it's only when viewed as a whole does the picture of Cyberpunk form as a wonderful world and subculture. Cyberpunk differs from many other flavours of subculture and fiction however. In the case of Cyberpunk the wisp that was a dream, that was a mere train of thought in the minds eye of technologist creatives, somewhere along the line, began to manifest in reality - like a snowball rolling down a mountain side turning into an avalanche.

The perception of a type movement in the past is false, but that doesn't matter - the movement happened none the less albeit in a much more subtle way.

The world imagined by the aesthetic and predicted technology of Cyberpunk is here in 2015. From fashions, the dystopian avant-garde politics, cyber warfare, hideous personal surveillance, the complete apathetic allowance and acceptance by the general public of both nation-state and corporations alike obvious (and amateur) erosions of individual privacy in the name of freedom and commerce and the corporate enslavement of all but the richest private citizens... and perhaps most importantly the role technology plays in our everyday lives; dominating them, sucking us into algorithms of big data and demographics. The future imagined by writers like William Gibson and Neal Stephenson (to name but two) have gradually become frighteningly prophetic as the snow ball gained momentum down the mountain of reality - to put it very succinctly, we're living in a 90's Cyberpunk Novel. No, really. We are.

We have sleep walked into dystopia. 2015. This is the age of Cyberpunk made real by technological advance and the decline of the nation state. The first world has seemingly embraced absolute corporatism, as the third world is left behind in a dark age of mismanaged philanthropy, exploitation and neglect - left to scavenge the scraps of advancement by the pseudo utopian oligarchs gifted near ultimate power by the ignorance of government in the past few decades who have let their own grasp on power be usurped by the march of the unholy alliance of corrupt big business and eager, hungry and naive talented technologists.

The human race appears to have stumbled the world and civilizations they created into a new social system, and not by mass consensus, indeed by mass apathy, where a technological elite now props up old world money and banking largely only for appearances sake. The post scarcity economy is coming. Automation is coming. AI is coming. And the lists of the have and have nots of this brave new world have already been drawn up by those turning the cogs and I doubt you are on the have list.

All those who chased after the colourful dragon and ultimate tech romance of the Cyberpunk future during the 90's are now getting to taste the dystopia we thought would be so cool - before we get to hand the crumbling, burning tech hell we've created to our children as the only existence they have ever and will ever know. Grim isn't it?

Unlike previous contemporary radical and revolutionary social movements from the 1950's, and in particular the much reminisced about 1960's (what did the hippy's actually achieve?) who dreamed and preached of change and revolution -my- generation actually achieved it through technology - bypassing governments and ideologies like deft ghosts in the shadows until it was too late to stop them. The world has changed forever due to the nerds, geeks, hackers, punks and phreaks of yesteryears basements.

Like all revolutions the change started small and ended bloody, dramatic and in no way resembling what those who instigated it actually wanted. And in this instance it may have ultimately destroyed life as we know it, and human freedom as we deserve it. Because it's true to say the only thing this the real Cyberpunk Era lacks from its embryonic speculative fiction predecessors is perhaps the most important element of those wonderful, inspiring stories which spawned it;

Resistance.

High tech, low life.

tl;dr Welcome to tech Hell.

You can escape.

Printed in Great Britain
by Amazon